NEW KID ON THE BLOCK

Copyright © 2025 By Lotus Soul Creative

ISBN 979-8-3194-5399-0 (Paperback)

All rights reserved. No part of this book may be reproduced without written permission of the copyright owner.

This book is dedicated to anyone who has ever felt like they don't belong.

To the reader,

May this book remind you to always be kind to everyone you meet, no matter how different they are.

1
Farewell Furry Friends

Kit woke abruptly to the usual combination of deafening meows and woofs with the odd howl and hiss, like a badly orchestrated choir. It usually put him in an instant grump of a mood, but not today. Today was different – a day he had waited what seemed like an eternity for. Today was his special day. The last day he had to wake up to that awful noise. It's not that he didn't feel grateful to be here – to have a place of safety, but it was far too crowded and noisy for his liking. Kit stretched his hind legs, surveying his chiselled claws, licking his grey-furred paws and feeling excited at the prospect of finally being free from the chaos of this place. Yes, that's right – Kit (don't mock the name – the 'creative' people at the rescue chose it!) was a free feline today! Finally, he was going to a place that he could call home.

He had spent his almost eight months of life here so hadn't ever experienced being in a proper home. He couldn't quite remember how he ended up here, but he had overheard the staff saying that he was found, along with his two brothers and sister, in a cardboard box dumped under a bridge. Not exactly the best start in life. One thing he could remember though, was that in the short time that they spent squashed together, starving and cold in that box, his brothers were mean to him just because he was the runt of the litter. He was thankful that his kind-hearted sister protected him and stood up to them. She held him tight during the cold and dark nights. Her love warmed him from the inside out and made him feel safe. She was like an angel but with fur, whiskers and claws (a feline version of an angel).

Fortunately, a woman on her morning run noticed the box and went to investigate. She got a real shock when it started moving so she looked inside to find them all in there huddled together.

They all ended up at Paw to Peace Animal Rescue run by a lovely couple called Mr and Mrs Saunderson. They had won a huge amount of money on the lottery so decided to use it to create the rescue five years ago – bless their cotton socks! The rescue itself is not a bad place at all, in fact, very lovely. Set amongst the stunning countryside, amazing, caring staff manned it. But it wasn't a home with a loving family so Kit was happy and incredibly excited to be moving on. He started to daydream about what his new home would be like and how it would feel to be loved and genuinely happy. He had manifested this day and played it out in his head so many times, imagining how wonderful his life would be.

"Well, don't you look like the cat that got the cream this morning?" a familiar voice jolted him from his thoughts.

It was Lilibet, an exquisite Persian with the most beautiful sea-green eyes you've ever seen and the smoothest silkiest fur you've ever rubbed up against. She had been Kit's neighbour at the rescue for the last couple of months and they had become good friends.

"Ahhhh, it's your release date today, isn't it?" she said, realising why he was smiling (which was unusual for him as he wasn't a morning cat).

"Sure is!" he replied with a huge cat that got the cream grin, "going to miss me?"

"Oh yes — let me see, what is there to miss? Your loud snoring and oh my goodness your butt — never smelt one like it!" she laughed.

They both giggled and had their last nose rub. Kit was happy to know that Lilibet's release date wasn't far away as a lovely family had met her yesterday and claimed her.

Kit packed his belongings in his suitcase – spare collar, flea spray and toy mouse – check!

"Hope that your new family treats you like the princess you are Lilibet," he said, as he prepared to vacate his room.

He was ready to go so he stepped enthusiastically into the cat carrier (for the first time ever as he knew he wasn't going to the dreaded vets this time). He stared through the gate at all the other animals, hoping it would be their turn soon.

"Farewell my furry friends!" he shouted.

"Keep your paws up – your turn will come soon!"

"Stay strong!"

2
Hello Happy Home

Through sleepy eyes, he spied a bright red front door edging closer. He had slept the whole journey – must have been the adrenaline from all the excitement.

DING DONG!

Kit almost jumped out of his fur!

What in the whiskers was that?!

A noise he'd never heard startled him and his tiny heart was beating so fast he thought it might pop out of his chest. This loud and unfamiliar sound jolted him instantly from his sleepy haze. He knew there were most likely more scares to come so he did some deep breathing to try and stay calm and grounded.

Suddenly, the door flung open. Kit could make out some legs, a green skirt and some pink, fluffy slippers– this was all he could see from the carrier. Then came a high-pitched voice which made him jump yet again.

"Oooooh, it's my new arrival!" the voice cooed excitedly.

The source of the voice crouched down and pushed their face up to the carrier which scared Kit (again), so he recoiled. It was a lady – she had kind, blue eyes, bright red lipstick, a cheery, wide smile and seemed nice enough, if not a little overexcited. Although nervous, Kit picked up a warm energy from her which made him feel a tinge of excitement for the new life ahead of him.

He felt hopeful that the lady lived alone as he didn't like young children much (they were far too boisterous for him). He remembered them visiting the rescue, banging, shouting and jumping up and down. He had hidden at the back of his pen hoping they wouldn't choose him. Thankfully, they didn't.

Kit passed the threshold of the house and that's when it hit him – not like a soft, comfortable pillow hitting you in the face but more like a large, heavy dumbbell smacking needed to stop being overdramatic and thinking the worst – it was no good worrying about something that might not even happen.

There was every chance that these resident cats could be lovely and welcoming and accept me as part of their family.

Kit continued trying to think positively to drown out any negative thoughts, whilst keeping his claws firmly crossed.

The lady (her name was Sheila) seemed pleasant enough and she scored major brownie points giving Kit some delicious, fresh tuna as a welcome treat. It was the best tuna he had ever tasted! He hadn't met the resident cats yet as he was just kept in one room, so he guessed this was the settling-in period he'd heard others talk about. He could smell them, so he knew they were there – he referred to them as them as because he had picked up more than one scent, and his nose had never let him down before.

Sheila wanted Kit to sit on her lap or next to her and looked sad that he chose to keep his distance. But he was exhausted and a little unsure of how to act, so he stayed in the carrier, which was kept open. He appreciated her making an effort, but he just needed some space to adjust to his new reality.

needed to stop being overdramatic and thinking the worst — it was no good worrying about something that might not even happen.

There was every chance that these resident cats could be lovely and welcoming and accept me as part of their family.

Kit continued trying to think positively to drown out any negative thoughts, whilst keeping his claws firmly crossed.

The lady (her name was Sheila) seemed pleasant enough and she scored major brownie points giving Kit some delicious, fresh tuna as a welcome treat. It was the best tuna he had ever tasted! He hadn't met the resident cats yet as he was just kept in one room, so he guessed this was the settling-in period he'd heard others talk about. He could smell them, so he knew they were there — he referred to them as them as because he had picked up more than one scent, and his nose had never let him down before.

Sheila wanted Kit to sit on her lap or next to her and looked sad that he chose to keep his distance. But he was exhausted and a little unsure of how to act, so he stayed in the carrier, which was kept open. He appreciated her making an effort, but he just needed some space to adjust to his new reality.

As he lay swathed in the soft, comfortable blankets that night, unable to sleep, he considered how lucky and blessed he was to finally find a home with a loving owner (and thankfully no noisy kids). He revelled in the silence of the night compared with the rescue. The only noise he could hear was the rhythmic tick-ticking of a clock, but that gave him a sense of calm as he found it rather soothing. He decided that he actually felt a little bit excited to meet the resident cats as he would have new friends, and at least he wouldn't get bored. He started counting mice jumping over cheese to help calm his mind and, eventually, fell into a deep sleep.

3
Cliquey Cats

A few days later, Kit was feeling a little more settled in his new home. Much to Sheila's delight, he had become more tactile, choosing to chill out on her lap more often. He enjoyed the warmth and especially getting lots of strokes. He really liked Sheila and appreciated her effort to connect with him. She had showered him with cat nip which made him feel super giddy and chilled out all at the same time. He had thoroughly enjoyed rolling around in it. She had also presented him with some kind of electronic gadget with a butterfly on the end that spun around over and over. That was lots of fun too. Life was good but, little did Kit know, that was about to change...

Something in the air felt different the following day. Kit's senses were on point and he knew that something was brewing. When Sheila left the door open, rather than close it as she usually did, his heart sank into the depths of his stomach as anxiety pulsed through his veins.
Today was the day — he felt it deep within his feline bones. He could smell their scents getting stronger and heard multiple paw patters drawing ever closer. He took deep breaths and reminded himself to think positively, trying to ignore the quickening of his heartbeat, repeating the affirmations in his head:

They will be welcoming and kind.

They will accept me into their clique.

He calmed his breathing and looked up at Sheila who was smiling down hopefully at him. The paw patters stopped momentarily and that's when he saw them for the first time. One, two, three... Kit counted them as all eyes locked onto him like lasers focused on their target. Kit gulped hard, feeling super nervous and evidently outnumbered.

"Now my lovelies, be nice, this is Kit," Sheila said.

She stood guard as the larger of the cats edged forward.

"This is Boris."

Boris was a pleasantly plump cat with long grey fur and huge paws. His eyes were wide and bright blue. Kit felt intimidated as those wide eyes pierced through him. He got the impression that Boris was the boss around here by the way he had confidently stepped forward. Boris gave a brief, forced smile whilst continuing to maintain intense eye contact that left Kit feeling a little uneasy.

"And these two are Amber and Sid," Sheila continued.

Kit looked at the other two residents. Sid was thin with fur as black as coal which made his yellow eyes seem brighter than they were. Again, a half-smile was all he got, but for that he was grateful. Amber was a beautiful tortoiseshell cat with gorgeous, wide, lime-green eyes and slender, elegant paws. She smiled at Kit radiating such a warm energy that enveloped him like meeting up with an old friend after many years apart. It seemed like an eternity that they all stood there. Kit didn't dare move – in fact, he felt frozen to the spot, all eyes still locked on him, surrounded by silence.

He knew that they wouldn't accept him straight away, but compared to how he had heard new meets could potentially go, it wasn't a complete disaster – or so he thought... As soon as Sheila left the room the whole energy changed as quick as a light switch being flicked. Boris came up close to Kit, almost nose to nose.

"So, what sort of a name is Kit?" he taunted.

"Ha ha, yeah, Kit Kat!" Sid laughed.

They both continued to laugh and surrounded Kit, circling him, looking him up and down. Kit gulped, feeling his anxiety rise, not knowing who to look at or how to respond. The situation didn't feel good at all and was less than welcoming.

"W-w-wasn't my choice," he stuttered.

"Where you from?" Boris quizzed.

"I lived at a rescue," Kit replied, in a voice so quiet he was surprised they heard him.

"Oh, my goodness! Not a rescue! Yuck! Wondered what that funny smell was," Sid said, looking at Kit in disgust.

"See, the thing is, we love Sheila, but we don't like to share. We can pretend to like you when she's around but make no mistake, *your sort* will never be welcome here," Boris said.

"Yeah, cos we are pure breeds and come from a quality line of feline ancestors," Sid boasted, "whereas I'm sure you were free or bought for a measly donation."

"Our sort does not mix with the likes of you, you see, that's just the way it is," Boris added.

"Talk about flexing your paws boys! He can't help where he's from and maybe he's okay," Amber interjected, much to Kit's relief. At least it seemed like someone was on his side.

"Shut up Amber! Remember your place. You're lucky we accepted you or shall we talk about where you're from?" Sid threatened.

"Erm, there's no need for that, I just thought we could give him a chance at least," she replied.

"No can do, it's feline law. It's written in the claws of royalty dating back years," Boris said proudly.

"You just made that up!" Amber replied, as both Boris and Sid giggled between themselves.

Kit felt knots in his stomach and wanted to say something but fear prevented him from speaking and, besides, what could he say? He couldn't change who he was or where he was from. Suddenly his new home didn't seem so appealing anymore and he dreaded what was ahead. But there was nothing he could do – he was stuck here. Just as Sheila headed back down the stairs, Boris whispered, "Watch your back," and resumed his position.

"Oh, hello my lovelies, looks like you're giving our new kit on the block a lovely welcome," Sheila observed, seemingly pleased with her resident clique.

She couldn't have been more wrong.

4
Bully Boys

Kit now had access to all areas of the house which should've been a positive thing, but it just left him feeling vulnerable. They now had access to him and were able to torment him. Thankfully, Amber didn't join in. After his introduction to the resident boys yesterday, he didn't dare encroach on their territory. He felt like a prisoner who had escaped prison only to find himself in another, which was far more dangerous. At least he'd felt safe at the rescue and had made friends with the residents. The only positive was that Amber, although a loose part of the trio, seemed much kinder and more accepting of him than the boys.

Kit was a peaceful cat who avoided confrontation at all costs, so fighting to find his place wasn't an option. Besides, he didn't fancy his chances against Boris's huge paws that no doubt contained even huger claws. All that time he'd waited for, longed for and dreamed of a home of his own and here he was stuck in a nightmare. The rescue now seemed more appealing — at least the resident cats didn't make him feel like he didn't belong. He had longed for freedom, but he was far from free in this house. The other cats dominated most areas, so he didnt dare wander too far. He didn't want any trouble, so he tried his best to stay out of their way. When it was feeding time he would hang back and wait for the others to finish, then check if the coast was clear before going to eat. Sometimes Boris would eat his food so he would be left to lick the bowl of what remained.

"Oh, Kit, you're such a shy boy," Sheila would say. If only she knew, but even if she did, what could she do?

He hadn't realised that being a rescue cat was such a terrible thing. It was through no fault of his own, and now he was paying for someone else's decision to put him in a box and abandon him. He started to feel like he wasn't good enough which is something he'd never felt before. It was affecting his self-confidence and made him feel utterly miserable. The next few days did nothing to ease these low feelings he was having.

Things just seemed to go from bad to worse. He was confined to one area of the house – the downstairs toilet, because wherever he went Boris and Sid would push him out of the way, chiming that it was their territory. Upstairs was definitely out of bounds as that's where they slept, so he didn't dare go up there.

Of course, when Sheila was around they acted friendly so she thought that everything was fine and dandy. If only she knew. Amber didn't join in with the bullying antics but was always in the background looking sympathetically at him. It was evident that she was under their control and perhaps she was doing what she needed to do to survive.

Kit had never felt so alone and unwanted in his life. He felt helpless and knew that nothing would change his situation. The boys pushed him to try and get him to fight but he ran off and hid in the toilet. He knew that he would lose the fight and end up severely injured. He hated to admit it, but he was scared. He wished he was stronger and hated himself for being so weak and not standing up to them. He thought the worst of it was over, but the worst was yet to come...

It was a Sunday afternoon, and Sheila had enjoyed a scrumptious roast beef dinner. Kit hadn't been eating much as all the worry had ruined his appetite. Besides, even when he tried to eat with the others, they shoved him out of the way and chased him. Sheila thought that they were just playing. The smell of the beef roasting had filled the house and Kit salivated at the delicious scent. All at once his appetite returned and his stomach churned with hunger. Sheila had kindly set aside some beef and gravy for her cats and Kit longed for a taste.

He waited impatiently for the others to finish eating. He hoped that they would leave him some, not like other times when they ate his share. But as they gathered around the food bowls, Kit was surprised when Boris shouted to him,

"Kit, there's some beef here for you!"

Kit felt excited and hungry, so he sprinted into the kitchen, full of hope.

Perhaps this was a peace offering from Boris.

Boris was stood next to a bowl full of delicious-smelling beef and gravy.

"Here you go, I left this for you as it's only fair," Boris said, smiling.

"Wow! Thank you so much Boris, that's so kind of you. I'm starving!" Kit replied, excitedly licking his lips as he approached the bowl.

Finally, he was invited to eat with them!

This was progress!

Perhaps this would turn out to be okay after all.

His heart skipped happily as he leaned down to devour the food. Suddenly, he felt a huge paw push the back of his head forward forcefully, then everything went black. As he raised his head back up all he could hear were the sounds of uncontrollable laughter from Boris and Sid.

"Ha Ha! Look at his face! HILARIOUS!" Sid laughed, rolling around on the kitchen floor.

"Oopsie daisy!" Boris teased, unable to stop laughing.

Kit struggled to see properly through the gravy stinging his eyes. It was dripping off his chin and whiskers, stuck in his fur and even up his nose. Kit sank to the floor feeling deflated and embarrassed. He realised that the joke was on him and that he had been foolish to think anything other. He wiped his eyes with his paws so he could see better, got up and walked back out of the kitchen. He walked past Amber who looked sad but never uttered as much as a meow, then past Boris and Sid, who were still laughing. Hungry and hurt, Kit returned to his place in the downstairs toilet and curled up, feeling lower than he ever had. He felt so stupid and unwanted, and any spark he had before today was well and truly distinguished. He had honestly believed that things might change, but instead it was all a cruel prank at his expense. As he lay there he realised that nothing would change. He cried himself to sleep, wondering what he had done to deserve this horrible life.

The next few weeks went by in a haze. Kit slept a lot as that was his only escape. Boris and Sid continued to make his life miserable, but he kept his distance as much as he could. He seldom came out of the downstairs toilet to the point that Sheila had started to worry about him, so she called the vet. Of course, the vet couldn't find anything wrong, as you can't detect or fix a broken spirit. But, unbeknownst to Kit, in the next few days something brilliant would happen that would give him a distraction and some much-needed freedom.

5
Fee-line Free

Just as Kit was ready to give up altogether, something brilliant happened that lifted his spirits. Sheila came and picked him up and placed him down at the back door, along with the others. She opened the door, and the others raced outside.

Kit hesitated as he felt uncertain of what was happening. The freshness of the gentle breeze hit his face as he took a cautious, slow step forward. He had never been outside in the big wide world before, having only been confined to a cardboard box and then the rescue.

"Go on Kit – don't be scared," Sheila said reassuringly.

Kit edged further forward until he was out of the door. He felt excited and nervous all at the same time, unsure of what lay ahead. The garden was spacious with neatly cut grass, some large potted plants, a huge tree at the end and high walls all around. That in itself was impressive so he couldn't imagine what lay beyond, but he was curious tofind out. The others were nowhere to be seen, for which he was thankful. He took a moment to breathe in the fresh air and felt the dark cloud of his existence lift just a little. For the first time since he'd arrived, he felt a rush of freedom run through his fur. He was free to explore the outside! Free to escape from the house that had become his prison, thanks to the bully boys. He had no idea of what to expect and knew that there might be dangers ahead, but he had to go for it, or he'd never know.

He reached the garden wall and jumped up to survey what was beyond. The garden led onto several alleyways leading to other streets with lots of houses — it was like a maze. Not knowing which way to go, he jumped down and cautiously set off to explore. One of the first things he picked up was the scent of other cats — he hoped they might be more friendly than his fellow residents. He didn't need any more drama in that respect. Gradually, excitement took over fear as he curiously roamed, loving his newfound freedom. Through alleyways he wandered, taking in the new scents — the smell of rubbish, dog poop and delicious food being cooked in the houses he passed by. He jumped up onto high walls and scaled fences, careful not to encroach onto anyone else's territory — he didn't want to make any more new enemies! He quickly learned that the outside world had its dangers, especially on the roads with cars zooming by. That gave him such a fright!

The roads were definitely not a safe place for cats to be.

Kit was so distracted by all the new sounds and smells overstimulating his brain that he didn't notice something approaching, until it was too late. He was suddenly startled by an unfamiliar scent and a panting sound close behind him that stopped him in his tracks. Kit froze, scared to turn around to see what it was. Curiosity getting the better of him, he slowly turned around to see a big, wet, black nose, a huge, wide mouth complete with razor-sharp teeth and a long, wet tongue dripping with saliva. It was so close to him that he could feel its breath on his fur.

Suddenly, a harsh, piercing sound he recognised as as bark jolted him from his frozen state into action, and he sprinted away as fast as his feline legs could carry him. Once at a safe distance and realising it wasn't following him, he looked back and realised it was dog with its owner. He was relieved to see that it was on a lead. Nevertheless, it had been far too close for his liking.

Maybe it just wanted to be friends.

It did look excited, but Kit wasn't experienced enough with dogs to be sure, so he wasn't sticking around to find out. He headed quickly back to the house which was safer than the uncertainty of the outdoors. He had had quite enough excitement for one day!

6
Nose Kisses

The next day, the rain poured down, much to Kit's disappointment. He had wanted to go back outside and away from the bad atmosphere in the house. He called it a house because it didn't feel like a home, or what he'd imagined a home to be like. His taste of freedom had given him a much-needed release. His hope that Boris and Sid would get bored after a time and would ease up on him faded, as it didn't look likely to happen anytime soon.

Kit was having a little snooze when he heard the door creak open. Startled, he looked up and was surprised to see Amber poking her pretty head inside.

"Ssssh," she whispered, putting her claw to her lips, "they're asleep upstairs"

She entered the room as Kit stretched, yawned and sat upright. He had to admit that he didn't trust her completely. He wondered if she'd been sent to play some sort of a prank on him, so he remained alert, as sadly his experience had taught him to be less trustful of others.

"Listen, I know you've been having a rough time with

them, but I wanted you to know that I'm not like them, and I think you're pretty cool actually."

"Erm… th… th… thank you, you too," Kit stuttered, feeling himself blush.

They chatted quietly (so as not to wake Boris and Sid) for a little while. Amber explained that she just wanted a quiet life and stuck with them so they wouldn't pick on her. She told how they had done the same to her when she arrived, teasing her because of her tortoiseshell pattern.

"But your tortoiseshell pattern is beautiful and unique," Kit reassured her, making her blush as she had done to him.

She told him that she felt bad for all they had done and that she had tried to get them to stop, but they never listened to her. Kit realised that she didn't have the power to make them change their ways, so she was in an awkward position. He appreciated that she had at least come to see him, even if she did have to sneak around behind their backs.

Before Amber scurried back upstairs, she rubbed noses with Kit, which was unexpected, but lovely. It made him feel all warm inside as it had been a while since he'd had nose kisses. In fact, the last time was from Lilibet when he left the rescue, and that was months ago.

He felt so relieved that at least someone was on his side in this house other than Sheila. Sheila had no idea what was going on, convinced by the friendliness they faked when she was around. It was when she left the room or, even worse, when she went out that they would start. Kit stayed in the living room on an evening as this is where Sheila watched TV, so he could get some much-needed peace and protection. This was his favourite part of the day, as it was the only time he could truly relax.

It may have poured down today, but Kit's heart was happy. He knew that Amber wasn't like the boys, and getting precious nose kisses made not being able to go outside bearable. He slept much better that night.

7
Alfie

The next day when Kit awoke, he noticed the sun streaming through the windows of the house, so he felt hopeful that he'd be able to go and explore outside again. After breakfast, Kit waited for the others to head out first whilst he stretched and basked in the warmth of the sunshine. Then he was off to explore again, a little wiser this time, making sure he stayed away from the roads and keeping his nose on high alert for any canine scents.

The sun had brought more people outside. He heard children playing and laughing in their gardens. At one point, some children approached him, which made him feel nervous and unsure. But he was relieved when he realised that these children were friendly and spoke to him in a soft, calm voice. This put him at ease so he allowed them to stroke him. He enjoyed that for a while before heading off. After all, who doesn't love extra strokes?

He was having a wonderful time when he came upon an area he hadn't seen before. It was a collection of houses arranged in a U shape — only six of them. Curiosity got the better of him, so he went to investigate. It was much quieter than the hustle and bustle of the alleyways, so he felt fairly safe and relaxed. He couldn't smell any canines and there was only one small road, so he set about having a little nosey around the gardens.

One garden, in particular, caught his attention where some brightly coloured flowers danced rhythmically in time to the light breeze, like a row of line dancers. He was busy having a good sniff when he became aware of a rather large shadow behind him. He turned around nervously to find another cat staring right at him. This cat was much larger than him, ginger, and had the same colour eyes as Kit. Kit was frozen in fear (again). He expected the cat to pounce on him so he poised himself ready to escape, if he could.

"EXCUSE ME! This is MY territory!" the cat shouted.

Kit gulped and backed away, realising that he had no chance against a cat of that size.

"Oh sorry…erm…listen…I don't want any trouble. I'll…erm…just go…please don't…" Kit stumbled with his words.

Before he could finish his sentence, the cat let out an almighty roar of laughter. Kit was confused but the cat couldn't stop laughing – so much so his eyes were leaking. Kit didn't know what to do. He wanted to run. He had no idea what was so funny. He was still half expecting this cat to pounce any second, so he remained frozen to the spot.

Eventually, the cat stopped laughing.

"Oh, you should've seen your face! I'm surprised your whiskers didn't fall off! the cat teased.

"I was just messing with ya silly. I mean, yeah, this is my territory, but I'm not a wannabe gangster like some of them around here. If you don't cause me any problems then I ain't got a problem with you."

Kit remained silent as he wasn't sure how to respond and was trying to drown out the sound of his heart beating so loudly.

"Hello!? Do you speak? Or has the cat got your tongue? Ha ha! Get it?" he started laughing again.

"Yeah, sorry, my name's Kit, I'm new around here, Kit

replied, finally able to speak.

"Ah well, my name's Alfie and I've lived here most of my life," he replied, holding out his paw to Kit.

They shook paws and Kit relaxed a little, hoping that Alfie was being genuine and not tricking him. He had given him such a fright.

"Wait! Kit?... Ha! So, you're the *new Kit on the block* then? he said, looking rather amused with himself.

"Guess I am," Kit replied, both of them laughing this time.

They chatted briefly but this was interrupted by a familiar voice shouting Kit's name in the distance.

"Great to meet you but I have to dash," Kit said, then headed home for his tea.

As he settled down that night, he smiled to himself, reflecting on what a brilliant day he'd had. Not even Boris and Sid teasing him could bring him down today. He'd met some nice children — he thought they were all noisy and horrible up until that point. He'd discovered some new areas and smelt some gorgeous, colourful flowers. But, more importantly, he thought that he may have just made his very first friend. He couldn't wait to see Alfie again. He prayed for pleasant weather for tomorrow and, hopefully, many more days to come.

8
Rescues United

Kit woke up happy. He immediately jumped up onto the window ledge to check outside and was relieved to see that it was another lovely day. He ate his breakfast quickly and, instead of waiting for the others, sped past them and headed out excitedly, as soon as the back door was open. Luckily, Kit was quick on his feet, so they had no chance of catching up with him, especially Boris.

He traced his way back to Alfie's house and loitered outside, hoping he would come out. He waited and waited but there was no sign of him. Disappointed, Kit sighed and was about to give up hope but, as he walked away, he heard him,

"Hey Kit Cat!"

Kit bounded excitedly over to Alfie.

"Hey, I've been waiting ages! I thought you weren't coming out."

"Ah sorry, it's the dreaded flea treatment day," Alfie said, "I tried to hide but he caught me, so forgive the smell."

They both lay in the sunshine chatting and grooming themselves. Alfie talked about his owner and how he was the only cat in the house, so he got lots of attention. Kit felt jealous, wishing he was an only cat — it sounded much less stressful than at his house.

"So, what's your home like?" Alfie enquired.

Kit's face dropped.

"What? It can't be that bad, surely?" Alfie asked, noticing the change in Kit's energy.

"Well, unlike you, I'm not an only cat. There are THREE others! My owner is lovely, but it's been horrible since I got there because of them."

"Why? What have they done?" Alfie asked.

Kit explained what had happened since he arrived — the pranks, the teasing and the boys isolating him. Alfie looked shocked and angry.

"Wow buddy, I'm sorry you've not had the best time. I don't understand why some cats behave like that, gives us all a bad name. Why they feel the need to bully you like that, I've no clue."

Kit continued talking about how terribly Boris and Sid had behaved, but just before he finished, Alfie interrupted,

"Wait! Hang on a minute, did you just say, Boris and Sid? As in them that live across the way, next to the park?"

"Yep! That's them. Why? Do you know them?" Kit asked

"I sure do, and they are known for causing trouble around here. So sorry you got lumbered with them, that's such bad luck."

Kit explained that the reason that they bullied him was because he came from a rescue centre. He noticed as he said this that Alfie became so angry his claws extended and his hackles were up.

"Alfie, what's up?" Kit asked, concerned.

"Well, just so you know, I'm from a rescue too and it boils my blood when anyone bullies someone for that," he said, through gritted teeth.

Alfie told Kit that he had had run-ins with both Boris and Sid. They had a history of fighting as they had tried to take over his territory. Alfie had taken them both on and they had gone running home with their tails between their legs. From that point on, they hadn't dared come near Alfie again. If they ever saw him, they would run in the opposite direction.

Kit would never have guessed that Alfie came from a rescue, but he was so glad he did, as it made him feel much less alone. He was a little worried at Alfie's response as he wasn't the sort of cat you wanted to get on the wrong side of. Kit was just relieved to be on his right side!

9
Cat Karma

Alfie had wanted to meet up around Kit's area the next day. Kit was unsure why, but agreed. So, when the others headed out, Kit met up with Alfie who was already at the bottom of the alleyway.

"Hey — you know what day it is today don't you?" Alfie asked excitedly.

"Erm... it's Wednesday, I think," Kit replied.

"Oh Kit, you have a lot to learn, look around you. What's different compared to a usual day in the alleyways?"

Kit surveyed the alley. The only thing that stuck out was the line of multiple black bins that weren't usually there.

"The bins?" Kit asked, unsure.

"YES! It's bin day! The best day of the week!"

"Why?" Kit asked, puzzled.

Alfie put his head in his paws.

"Oh, Kit, bless your pretty paws, you remind me of myself when I was younger, it's time for a good old rummage – watch and learn!"

Alfie jumped up onto one of the bins and managed to tip it over, which made Kit jump. All the rubbish spilled into the alley and, in an instant, Alfie was headfirst into it, ripping open bags. He lifted his head out and looked over at Kit,

"Well, come on then! Get stuck in!"

Kit joined him and quickly learned how much fun it was. How they laughed, especially when Kit got a banana skin stuck on his head! This was the most fun he had ever had. He even managed to find a half-eaten chicken that him and Alfie shared.

They decided to try another bin but, just as Alfie started to rummage, Kit heard a familiar but unwelcome voice behind him.

" Ewww! Look at the smelly rescue rummaging in the smelly bins!"

It was Boris and Sid. They were both laughing so hard that they didn't notice Alfie approaching them. They hadn't seen him as he was at the bottom of the bin. When they realised, it was too late for them to escape. Alfie towered over the pair as the colour drained from their fur and they cowered, shaking.

"O...oh...A...A...Alfie, didn't see you there," Boris stuttered.

"So, what was that you just said about smelly rescues? What's wrong with rescue cats?"

"Oh... well... come on Alfie, you know that us pure breeds don't mix with *their sort*," Sid replied.

Kit noticed Amber appear and, upon hearing what Sid said, she rolled her eyes and shook her head. Alfie took a deep breath and moved ever closer to the terrified pair until he was right in their faces.

"Really? Hmmmm," Alfie paused, adding to the tension in the atmosphere, "you do know that *I'm* a rescue cat like my good friend Kit over there? I'm very proud of it, by the way."

Boris and Sid's mouths were wide open as they both attempted to talk over each other, stuttering and grovelling to Alfie. Kit had to hold in his amusement at seeing them squirm so much. Amber seemed to be feeling the same as he noticed her also trying not to laugh. Alfie flexed his big paws, surveying his super-sharp claws and hissed loudly. Boris and Sid fell backwards, begging Alfie not to hurt them and apologising over and over. But Alfie was not backing down and marched them over to the bin.

He forced them into it and he, Kit and Amber pushed the bin back up, closing the lid. All three of them then burst into fits of laughter, rolling around the alleyway ground.

"Can I hang with you guys? Please? I've had enough of those two," Amber asked, once they had all managed to stop laughing.

"Of course you can, sweet cheeks," Alfie replied, with a wink.

They three of them headed to the field to chase some mice, leaving Boris and Sid banging and pleading to be let out of the smelly bin.

After chasing mice for a few hours, Amber and Kit headed home for tea, with the boys nowhere in sight. The house was quiet without them so Kit enjoyed it and, for once, ate his food in peace, without having to look over his shoulder.

Later in the evening, Boris and Sid finally arrived back home but what a sorry state they were in. Boris had potato peel stuck in his fur and Sid had a plaster stuck to his forehead! They were both filthy and stinking.

"Where on earth have you two been?! Look at the state of you!" Sheila exclaimed disapprovingly.

Amber and Kit giggled between themselves, feeling very amused indeed. Boris and Sid approached them looking sheepish and embarrassed. Kit thought that they might seek revenge, blaming him for what had happened, but he was wrong.

"Kit, look, we're sorry," Sid said.

"Yeah, we were only messing with you," Boris added, trying to make out it had all been one big joke.

"Ewwww, what's that smell?" Amber teased, not able to contain her giggles.

"Smells like a smelly pure breed to me," Kit laughed.

Boris and Sid didn't look happy at all and sulked all evening, feeling very sorry for themselves, especially when Sheila had to bath them. This just added to Kit and Amber's amusement even more.

"This day just keeps getting better and better," Amber said.

"It sure does! Karma is a wonderful thing," Kit agreed.

That night, for the first time, Kit and Amber slept upstairs huddled together, and Kit had the best sleep ever.

10
Happy Home Ever After

Thanks to Alfie, everything changed for Kit from that day on. Boris and Sid couldn't have been nicer if they tried. Of course, he knew it was only out of fear of Alfie, but he didn't care. He was finally free to go wherever he wanted in the house and able to relax, which is how it should've been from the start. He was finally experiencing what it was like to live in a happy home. No longer did he have to hide in the downstairs toilet and be afraid of them. He could now refer to the house as a home — his home. Life was good.

Although they had made his life miserable, he wasn't going to do the same to them as two wrongs don't make a right and, besides, it wasn't in Kit's nature. He had accepted their apology, but he wouldn't forget. He was friendly with them for the sake of keeping the peace and harmony in the house. He felt that they were suffering enough anyway, as they were constantly in fear of bumping into Alfie again, so that was their consequence. He just hoped that they would learn their lesson, but time would tell.

Kit was focused on living his best life, spending time with his BFFs, Alfie and Amber, and continuing to be the kind, friendly feline he had always been. Days turned into weeks that turned into months and life continued to be good for Kit. He had his freedom, happiness, awesome friends, a loving owner, exploring the neighbourhood, chasing mice and not forgetting the weekly bin day! What more could a feline want?

Then one day that seemed like any other day, Kit became aware of a new cat scent in the house. He noticed that the front room door, which was usually open, was closed for a few days. Something was occurring, that he knew to be true.

The next morning, he woke up to Sheila calling them all, so he stretched, yawned a big yawn, and followed Amber downstairs to the living room. He noticed that the door was now open and, when he entered, he saw the most adorable, blue-eyed, young cat with beautiful sand-coloured fur sitting in the middle of the room. He was visibly trembling and looked terrified. Kit recalled how he had felt when he first met the resident cats, leading to a sense of empathy towards the new arrival.

"This is Kit," Sheila said.

"This is our new rescue, Timber."

Boris, Sid, and Amber were already in there. Kit stepped forward and smiled, noticing the instant relief appear on the new little feline's face.

As soon as Sheila left the room, Kit eyeballed Boris and Sid, who looked away nervously. There was no way he was going to let history repeat itself. He knew they wouldn't dare, especially as they now knew that Alfie was a rescue cat too.

"Hi Timber, I'm from a rescue too, welcome to your new home. Stick with me and you'll be just fine," Kit reassured the new resident.

MORALS OF THE STORY

Always be kind.
Accept everyone, even if they are different.
Bullying is not cool.
We are all unique.
Two wrongs don't make a right.

REFLECTION TIME

💭 Describe a time when you were kind to someone.

💭 When was someone kind to you? How did it make you feel?

💭 If you met someone new, what would you do to make them feel welcome?

💭 If you or someone else was being bullied, what would you do?

💭 Do you think that someone should be treated differently if they are different? Why?

💭 How are you different from others?

💭 Is being different a good thing? Why?

Acknowledgements

Thanks to my fabulous friend, Lou, for helping me to keep believing in myself and to keep going when self-doubt crept in.

Thanks to my amazing parents for always supporting me, especially when I need it the most.

Lastly, thanks to my gorgeous fur babies, Bruno and Bella, for existing, and making every day just that little bit brighter with their unconditional love.

About the Author

Lotus Soul Creative was created by Kerry Fisher to share her passion for art and writing. Kerry is an ex primary school teacher living in Cumbria with her two cats (certified crazy cat lady!) and is a Mum of two boys. Alongside writing and creating art, she enjoys spending time in nature, singing, acting and music.

ALSO AVAILABLE (via Amazon):

'Did You Know? Exploring the Wonder of Animals Through Poetry' – poems containing interesting animal facts for ages 7-11 with quizzes and learning activities.

'Animaltastic' – artwork framed by short animal poems – age 7+.

'WOW! Animals!' – animal rhyming sentences for 5-6 year olds with activities to help reading and writing.

Contact Kerry via email: lotussoulcreative@gmail.com

Printed in Great Britain
by Amazon